Praise for *Dro*

Invigorating! Throughout my experience as a therapist, most issues are closely related to the person's self-image and early social interactions. In this book, Michael Mines illustrates this and stimulates the mind and the emotions. His biblical insight and encouragement will strengthen and help lead women to begin to look at the emotional wounds of life experiences and step through the threshold of inner healing. Everyone that reads this book will find hope in and freedom through Christ.

- *Sherry R. Calhoun, MA (Mental health therapist)*

This book has reminded me how great it is to be a woman and has challenged me to keep pushing forward!

- *Cassandra Ayers, Assistant Manager of The Avenue & single mother*

Calling all women: this book is a must read! it carries a yoke-destroying anointing.

- *Apostle Harriett Askew, Wilderness Christian Alliance*

This book is AWESOME because it speaks to your soul and spirit. I would suggest this writing for study in all women ministries and conferences.

- Minister Cherie Holloman, Assistant Pastor, Triumph in Victory Christian Center

Dropping Your Waterpots

How to Live Life without Lack, Labels, or Loneliness

By Michael Mines

Published by Aardvark Global Publishing
9587 So. Grandview Dr.
Salt Lake City, UT 84092

© by Michael Mines, 2008
ISBN-13: 978-1519490711
ISBN-10: 1519490712

All rights reserved. No portion of this book may be reproduced, stored in a retrieval system, or transmitted in any form or by any means—electronic, mechanical, photocopy, recording, scanning, or other—except for brief quotations in critical reviews or articles, without the prior written permission of the author.

All Scripture quotations, unless otherwise indicated, are taken from the King James Version of the Holy Bible. Scriptures marked NKJV are taken from the New King James Version.

Copyright ©1982 by Thomas Nelson, Inc.
Used by permission. All rights reserved.

This book is dedicated to my mother
Sharon Annette Mines

Thanks, Mom, for keeping your baby out of jail, off the streets, and in the church.

Notes

CONTENTS

Forward i
Preface vii
The Word 1
    John 4:7-29 3

The Woman 5
    Getting to Know Her 7
Her Self-Esteem 9
    Accepting the label 11
    Mark downs attract bargain hunters 17
    It's a jungle out there 21
    Removing the labels 22
    You're still fab! 26
    Timing isn't Everything 29

Her World View 31
    ABC'S & 123'S 33
    Just Answer the Question 36
    Who died and left you in charge? 40
    Knowing who you are 41
    Supply and Demand 44
    Daddy's little girls 47
    Women believe me! 53

Her Relationships 57
    Oh Well; You've got your reasons 58
    Who's filling you? 62
    Family matters? 64
    Check your crowd 67
    Exit Stage Right 69

You've Got Mail	71
While you were sleeping	77
This is not what I bargained for	79
Letting go	83
I built my world around ___?	87
Dropping Your Waterpot	91

About the Author	94
Acknowledgements	95

Foreword

By Ebony Jackson
Editor–in–Chief, Forward Press Publishing

Never have I been more honored than I am right now. When I was originally approached to write the foreword for *Dropping Your Waterpots* I was absolutely ecstatic. I was so humbled that a friend, a brother, and a co-worker who I hold in such high regard would actually ask that I lend my thoughts, my time, and my words to such an endeavor. As I waited for the text to be given to me, I thought about all of the intellectual and thought provoking conversations and the laughter that has been shared between Mike and me over lunch breaks and free time. As I continued to sit and think about the man that he is, even being a writer and publisher in my own right I still began to feel intimidated as though I were unworthy to write the foreword for a book of such magnitude. I expressed my fears to him and he simply brushed them aside and assured me that I was just the person for the job. On the day that the text was given to me, upon seeing the title, I asked him what the nature of the book was. I was well aware that it was of a spiritual/religious nature, but I wanted to know what vice in particular he was attempting to tackle. He was very vague (which I now believe was intentional) as he informed me that it was based on a message that he preached sometime before and had since been led to expand the message into book form. I accepted the answer Mike provided and at the end of the day, I gathered the manuscript along with the rest of my belongings for the drive home. After parking my car, I reached for the manuscript lying on the passenger seat. There was a gentle breeze, the pages fluttered and turned. As they came to rest what I saw were the words, "Getting to Know Her." Being the inquisitive person that I am, I asked myself aloud who is this "her"? Then, I began to read, and "her" became very apparent. It's true. We all know her. We are all aware of the woman who spends countless hours online scrolling through websites or spends her weekends haunting the aisles of her neighborhood bookstore in search of books written by self-help gurus that promise to show her how to totally reinvent herself in 30 days or less. She is drawn like a moth to a flame towards a magazine that will supposedly lift the veil of mystery and reveal to her the top ten ways that she can tell whether or not the man in her life truly loves her. I thought about how she spends almost every waking moment of her life changing and compromising herself for the gratification of someone who does not truly know her or if he does he remains unimpressed and uninterested. Listen to her as she cries, beats herself up, and declares all the changes that she would make to herself and her life if she just had the chance. After listening to her heartache, you slowly watch her become bitter and blame every man she has ever come across for all of her problems, all of her setbacks, and as she vows that she will never again be anyone else's doormat, you instantly begin to feel this combustible combination of pity and anger for her because you know that in a month's time, you will be sitting in her living room or her dining room listening to the same story again and although she is still playing the role of the damsel in distress, there is a new cast member who has been selected to play her leading man. He is scripted to play the role of Prince Charming, but will only be remembered for his standout performance as the evil villain.

As you sit and think about how many times you have heard this story and as you listen to her endless banter, you somewhat tune her out as you begin to search within yourself to try and find some words of encouragement that you can offer her that she may not have heard before or even some that she may have forgotten. As you struggle to find the words of motivation, you become angry with yourself that you continue to allow her to poison your ears and vex your spirit with her never-ending, sordid tales of love gone awry. Right before you stand to your feet with your hands balled into fists and gather your courage to tell her that you can no longer idly sit by and listen to her any further. You sit back down as you come to the realization, She is you.

As the recognition begins to permeate every fiber of your being, you begin to interrogate yourself. Am I really her? When did I become her? Does anyone else know that I am her? If so, why didn't they tell me? After debating these questions for hours, you begin to realize that as her, you arenot yet equipped to answer any of these questions on your own. After all, if you were, why didn't you know you were "her" in the first place? It is then that you understand that it is going to take a lot more than a few self-help books and advice from your friends to get you through this ordeal. You have no choice but to prepare yourself to not conquer this with mere flesh and blood, but with the Spirit of God. With choosing fight for your life and sanity in the spiritual realm, you may ask the question, where do I begin? As with any great story of triumph, you start at page one.

There are no words to describe the power and the healing that can be found on the pages of *Dropping Your Waterpots*. As an author Mike Mines brilliantly constructed a text that does more than call the mental, emotional, and spiritual troubles that women face to the forefront. In *Dropping your Waterpots* he also provides you with realistic resolutions (no quick fixes) followed by God's word as confirmation. Not only is it rare that this is done, but it is also rare that healing, self-love, and progression are made so simple. In the pages that follow, you will find it impossible to not only desire transformation for yourself, but also desire that same transformation for your sister, your mother, or your cousin.

As previously stated, when I initially asked Mike what the book was in reference to, he was intentionally unclear on the subject matter. I now believe it was because he knew that I was the "her" he was writing about. By forcing me to read the material on my own, he forced me to revisit myself and he made me responsible for the change that I needed and now know that I have always deserved. Anyone who is truly willing to search their hearts and their innermost thoughts to discover the true "her", to see what labels she carries, how she has devalued herself, what she has built her world around, and how to let it all go and drop her waterpots, there is no better place to start than with this book. And there is no better time to start than today.

Notes

Introduction

You know her…She is your sister, your aunt, she is your cousin once or twice removed. She is the black sheep of the family. She is that friend. You know the one. She's the chat of the church, the water cooler "what now" the Laundromat listen up", or the "community conversation." The one who always seems to live life so far left of center. Her romantic misadventures are always providing the "Hush Yo' Mouth" stories at family barbeques. You know her. She's the biblical poster child for the woes of divorce and remarriage. She may even be you. She is "The Woman at the Well," or so we call her. The irony of this title is that she desperately longed to disassociate herself from the very well of which we refer. You may say the well is how we know her; otherwise she would just be 'The Woman" right? Well, (no pun intended) consider this. Is it really fair to say you know this woman if you don't know her name?

Can I presume to know you based on the infamy or notoriety of one publicized event in your life? Shall I say I know you based on the random churnings of a rumor mill? Of course not, still, like so many women today she is labeled; her reputation forever marred in the annals of biblical history as well as in the minds of contemporary Christians 2000 years removed. Often, when the Bible speaks of knowing someone there is a deeper level of intimacy involved. For instance, Genesis 4:1 says, "And Adam knew Eve his wife; and she conceived, and bare Cain, and said, I have gotten a man from the Lord."

Intimacy is taking the time to look beyond the surface to see the heart of an individual. True intimacy should ultimately give birth to a deeper understanding and appreciation at the core of who one is. It is my prayer that this visit with her will be an intimate encounter; I pray that this spiritual rendezvous gives birth to the understanding that her life and story offers more than a chastening finger against remarriage or promiscuity. She is more than an icon for any dogmatic or theological platform. At the end of the day she is "Every Woman;" fearfully and wonderfully made. She is more than the sum of a few broken relationships. We will examine what I believe are the three dimensions of her struggle, Her self-esteem, Her world view and then her relationships. As we examine these three dimensions it will become apparent that the husbands for which she is remembered were not her struggle but symptoms of other problems not seen from the surface. I suspect that like her there is more to you than meets the eye.

One's failed relationships and bad decisions however numerous, are not the primary target areas for healing but are collateral damage caused by the fall out of deeper conflicts. As you read this book, I pray that you in some way are able to identify with her; If not with her specific struggles, then with the universality of struggle itself. (We all have them) Only then can we truly rejoice in her triumphs and even celebrate them as our own. Finally, my hope is that you might draw from the fountain of living water that still flows from her story.

Notes

The Word

John 4:7-29 (New King James Version)

7 A woman of Samaria came to draw water. Jesus said to her, "Give Me a drink."

8 For His disciples had gone away into the city to buy food.

9 Then the woman of Samaria said to Him, "How is it that You, being a Jew, ask a drink from me, a Samaritan woman?" For Jews have no dealings with Samaritans.

10 Jesus answered and said to her, "If you knew the gift of God, and who it is who says to you, 'Give Me a drink,' you would have asked Him, and He would have given you living water."

11 The woman said to Him, "Sir, You have nothing to draw with, and the well is deep. Where then do you get that living water?

12 Are You greater than our father Jacob, who gave us the well, and drank from it himself, as well as his sons and his livestock?"

13 Jesus answered and said to her, "Whoever drinks of this water will thirst again,

14 but whoever drinks of the water that I shall give him will never thirst. But the water that I shall give him will become in him a fountain of water springing up into everlasting life."

15 The woman said to Him, "Sir, give me this water, that I may not thirst, nor come here to draw."

16 Jesus said to her, "Go, call your husband, and come here."

17 The woman answered and said, "I have no husband." Jesus

said to her, "You have well said, 'I have no husband,'
18   for you have had five husbands, and the one whom you now have is not your husband; in that you spoke truly."
19   The woman said to Him, "Sir, I perceive that You are a prophet.
20   Our fathers worshiped on this mountain, and you Jews say that in Jerusalem is the place where one ought to worship."
21   Jesus said to her, "Woman, believe Me, the hour is coming when you will neither on this mountain, nor in Jerusalem, worship the Father
22   You worship what you do not know; we know what we worship, for salvation is of the Jews.
23   But the hour is coming, and now is, when the true worshippers will worship the Father in spirit and truth; for the Father is seeking such to worship Him.
24   God is Spirit, and those who worship Him must worship in spirit and truth."
25   The woman said to Him, "I know that Messiah is coming" (who is called Christ). "When He comes, He will tell us all things."
26   Jesus said to her, "I who speak to you am He."
27   And at this point His disciples came, and they marveled that He talked with a woman; yet no one said, "What do You seek?" or, "Why are You talking with her?"
28   The woman then left her waterpot, went her way into the city, and said to the men,
29   "Come, see a Man who told me all things that I ever did. Could this be the Christ?"

The Woman

Getting to Know Her

You know her…She is your sister, your aunt, she is your cousin once or twice removed. The proverbial black sheep of the family. She is that friend. You know the one; she is the chat of the church, the water cooler "what now" the laundromat "listen up", or the "community conversation." The one who always seems to live life so far left of center. Her romantic misadventures are always providing the "Hush Yo' Mouth" stories at family barbeques. You know her. She's the biblical poster child for the woes of divorce and remarriage. She may even be you. She is "The Woman at the Well," or so we call her. The irony of this title is that she desperately longs to disassociate herself from the very well of which we refer. You may say the well is how we know her; otherwise she would just be 'The Woman" right? Well, (no pun intended) consider this. Is it really fair to say you know the woman if you don't know her name? Can I presume to know you based on the infamy or notoriety of one publicized event in your life? Shall I say I know you based on the random churnings of a rumor mill? Of course not, still, like so many women today she is labeled; her reputation forever marred in the annals of biblical history as well as in the minds of contemporary Christians 2000 years removed.

Often, when the Bible speaks of knowing someone there is a deeper level of intimacy involved.

For instance, Genesis 4:1 says, *"And Adam knew Eve his wife; and she conceived, and bare Cain, and said, I have gotten a man from the LORD."* Intimacy is taking the time to look beyond the surface to see the heart of an individual. True intimacy should ultimately give birth to a deeper understanding and appreciation at the core of who one is. It is my prayer that this visit with her will be an intimate encounter; I pray that this spiritual rendezvous gives birth to the understanding that her life and story offers more than a chastening finger against remarriage or promiscuity. She is more than an icon for any dogmatic or theological platform. At the end of the day she is "The Woman;" fearfully and wonderfully made. This one factor makes her more than the sum of a few broken relationships. You will see that her struggle is three dimensional. The husbands for which she is remembered are not her struggle but are symptoms of her struggle.

This woman's failed marriages, however numerous, are not the enemy's primary target but are collateral damage caused by the fall out of an internal conflict. As you read this book, I pray that you in some way are able to identify with her; If not with her struggles, then certainly her triumphs. Finally, my hope is that today you might draw from the fountain of living water that still flows from her story.

Her Self-esteem

Accepting the Label

"My brethren, have not the faith of our Lord Jesus Christ, the Lord of glory, with respect of persons. For if there come unto your assembly a man with a gold ring, in goodly apparel, and there come in also a poor man in vile raiment; And ye have respect to him that weareth the grand clothing, and say unto him, Sit thou here in a good place; and say to the poor, Stand thou there, or sit here under my footstool: Are ye not then partial in yourselves, and are become judges of evil thoughts?" (James 2: 1-4).

What is a label? A label is defined as a word or phrase used to describe a person or group. It is a piece of paper, fabric, or plastic attached to \something to give instructions about it or identify it.

Labels are an integral part of sales and marketing. Every company strives to achieve brand name recognition. From breakfast cereals, to cars and electronics, highly paid marketing executives are constantly looking to create a label that says 'must have' to the consumer. Given five seconds you would most assuredly be able to rattle off two or three labels that were once at the height of fashion or on the cutting edge of pop culture, but are now passé. The labels didn't change, only your perception of them. This ever changing market culture in which labels rise and fall everyday may work just fine for designers of fashion. However, to the person having to live life with a label, constantly searching for the approval of the masses or waiting for perceptions to sway in his favor becomes an emotional roller coaster that will ultimately end with the person being disappointed. In an open market society, approval is too conditional, and perceptions are often fleeting. It is in this aggressive marketing culture that I have learned and would like to share some important life lessons. I've spent more than a decade in the sales and marketing business. You name it, and I've probably sold it. Water treatment systems, vacuums, women's apparel, magazines, software, internet access and timeshare have all been pitched by yours truly. Out of all the products I've sold, I learned more about life and people while selling timeshare than in all the other industries combined. Perhaps because the selling process is longer, timeshare often requiring me gain an understanding of a buyer's hopes and dreams, goals and priorities. I must have spent hours conversing with potential buyers about things that had nothing at all to do with timeshare. I sold timeshare in beautiful resorts, and in rundown hotels. Through the selling of timeshare I have been blessed with the opportunity to deal with men and women from all walks of life and of every age group and income level. I've dealt with men and women of various nationalities and of every sexual orientation. I sat across a table from and conversed with baby boomers and Woodstock attendees. Pastors, Priest, witches, Jehovah witnesses and atheists have all shared a little piece of themselves with me. I have dined with garbage men engineers and athletes, all in the name closing a deal.

> We are constantly selling and marketing ourselves every day in one aspect or another.

However, more than anything else, the negotiating has helped me to understand the need for value, standard and price, and the why's and how's of raising and lowering them. Now, if it sounds as though I am a great salesman or that I have amassed a fortune or become a guru of some sort, I haven't. I was only moderately successful most of the time. However it is not from my success that my wisdom has been gleaned, but my failures and the understanding of why I failed. You may not yet understand how labels and marketing affect your life beyond the various products and services that you buy. The mere implication of selling one's self may even offend your feminine psyche as it may at first conjure images of seedy hotels, street corners, or brothels. Still, looking beyond such negative connotations, we are all constantly selling and marketing ourselves every day in one aspect or another. Have you ever said to someone "Don't sell yourself cheap?" Have you ever described someone or something as "a dime a dozen?" If so, you have applied marketing lingo to ordinary people and circumstances. For this cause I am convinced that as we peel away the many layers of this woman's complexities you will agree that my use of sales and marketing as an analogy about life is not a stretch; but a very real synopsis.

In verse 7, Jesus initiates a conversation by saying to the woman, "Give me a drink." It seems like a simple enough request. However, she finds it to be confusing. She cannot understand why Jesus is speaking to her or believe that he might actually want anything she has to offer. "Then the woman of Samaria said to Him, 'How is it that You, being a Jew, ask a drink from me, a Samaritan woman?' For Jews have no dealings with Samaritans" (John 4:9). She is in essence directing his attention to her label because it identifies and offers instructions on how to handle her. She reminds him that her label is that of a Samaritan woman, and that it comes with the following instructions: Samaritans are inferior, illegitimate and are to be treated as such. According to the Bible history, Samaritans were considered a bastard race of illegitimate Jews. This label is even more devastating to this woman, because as a woman she is least even among those considered least of all. Understand that how she sees herself as an individual ultimately sets the value that she places on herself and her potential. Somewhere along the way, the woman accepted the labels that society placed on her. Her perception is her reality and is severely limiting her capacity for growth. Clearly this woman is a slave in her thinking, hopelessly resigning to live a life of bondage on the plantations of her own ethnicity, gender, identity and status. Given her response, she expects to be ignored or overlooked. She is not thinking that Jesus can see beyond her labeling. After all, she cannot; and how could she, when the very times in which she lives demand labels such as Jew, Greek, bond or free, circumcised or uncircumcised. Hers is a time not unlike our own in which labels can make you or break you, open doors, or slam them shut.

Think about it for a moment, how many times are you willing to pay more for a purse than it is actually worth simply because of its label? You don't care that it was quickly thrown together in some offshore sweat shop for little or nothing. It may not even be the real thing but it has the right label, so you buy it. Or, in sharp contrast, how many times do you pass by the little kiosk in the mall? The owner still uses the finest materials and hand stitches every purse with care, each one an original that only you will have. You are not moved by the amount of time and energy put into making these bags, neither are you impressed by the vender's choice of quality over lowering his overhead. His bags are surely worth every penny of the asking price, but they have the wrong label so you keep walking. Not having the right label in a label obsessed society eventually forces that vender to drastically lower his prices just to get a buyer's attention and stay in business. At first, lowering his prices hurts because he does not make a profit. However, he notices that they do sell, so the next time, in order to make a profit, he lowers his overhead by cutting a few corners. He lowers his standards on quality and materials, doesn't spend as much time and effort as before. This way, the quality of his purses now matches the lowered price. He has sacrificed value, price, quality and standard to conform to the market. *"Do not be conformed to the things of this world" (Romans 12:22)*. Instead of lowering his standard to fit the market, he can move his kiosk to another location where the market is different, or non-existent. At this point the market can be his to create. My question to you is this: has being labeled caused you to lower the standards in some area your life? Are you compromising your values in order to remain in a market that doesn't want you the way you are? What corners of your life have you cut? Take the time to do an analysis of yourself and your current market. You may find that the market you're in is not where you belong. *"Now the LORD had said unto Abram, Get thee out of thy country, and from thy kindred, and from thy father's house, unto a land that I will show thee: And I will make of thee a great nation, and I will bless thee, and make thy name great; and thou shalt be a blessing" (Genesis 12:1-2)*.

Mark downs attract bargain hunters

> *"They hunt our steps, that we cannot go in our streets: our end is near, our days are fulfilled; for our end is come. Our persecutors are swifter than the eagles of the heaven: they pursued us upon the mountains, they laid wait for us in the wilderness" (Lamentations 4:18-19)*

In the timeshare industry, I've learned that the ability to handle time and rejection separates the strong closers from the weak. Time and rejection; or rejection over time if not overcome will cause a weak seller to fall into what I call a pitiful mark down. A pitiful mark down is the lowering of price because true value is not translated by the closer or perceived by the customer.

The pitiful mark down is much like this woman's low self esteem in that it doesn't happen immediately. There is a slow but steady decline into the pit of low self-esteem. As a closer, I was never weakened by the first customer or the first no of the day. I knew that there were more tours lined up and somebody was going to buy. That was eight o'clock in the morning. Eight hours and a few no's later, I wasn't nearly as confident. Rejection over time had gotten the best of me. Exhausted, desperate, and unable to handle another turndown, I was ready to give away every luxury week of vacation I could. The buyers were selling the seller. Let down after let down convinced me that what I had to offer was not as valuable as I thought. The fear of going home without a sale would set in. I would decide at that point to say whatever I needed to say get a sale, I would not hold my prices so high again; that might chase the next buyer away like the others. I decided that I was going to accept any offer the next buyer made.

This time I would lower my value, my standards and my price. After hearing no so many times, I was thirsty for a yes. Even if I felt in my heart that I was sacrificing too much! Hearing someone say yes now would feel so right that I would just have to deal with my conscience later. The decision to undergo a pitiful mark down begins in the mind. It then finds a place in the heart. Finally, the signs go up in the eyes — which are the windows of the soul. Whenever a woman falls into a desperate state of mind, she begins to attract bargain hunters. Smelling her fear of rejection and sensing her desperation, bargain hunters prepare to pounce. They will then make offers based on her fear rather than the true value off what she has to offer. Her gifts, her time, her anointing and her body are each consumed. All that

> A designer's original, hand made by God himself, finds her self esteem on the clearance racks of life, or in the bargain bins of relationships; constantly being rummaged through by those who want something for nothing.

is left is the carcass of a once vibrant woman now spiritually, physically, and emotionally mauled beyond recognition. Consider the term "bargain hunter". Wherever there is a hunter, there must also be prey. The hunter scouts his prey from some unseen location, and waits patiently for the right moment to strike. "The wicked watcheth the righteous, and seeketh to slay him" (Psalm 37:32). Bargain hunters never seek those who are strong. Instead, they look for labels that identify a woman as slightly irregular, used, as is or damaged goods. Regardless of what labeling a woman has accepted, the results are the same. A designer's original, hand made by God himself, finds her self esteem on the clearance racks of life, or in the bargain bins of relationships; constantly being rummaged through by those who want something for nothing. Could it be that you or someone close to you has undergone a pitiful mark down? Have values, standards, and goals been lowered to gain acceptance? Are you ever tempted to down play your intelligence for fear of intimidating other people? Do you pretend to be needy because your independence fails to stroke someone's male ego?

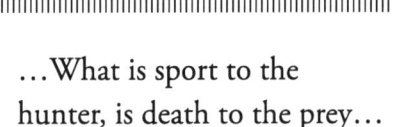

...What is sport to the hunter, is death to the prey...

Sadly many women today have marked themselves down due to the accepting of labels or to accommodate the insecurities of others. Labels have a way of distorting the truth by hiding even the slightest indications of who a woman truly is or what she is actually worth. Without these truths it is easy to become lost. Desperate and unsure of themselves, many fall prey to bargain hunters. There are those who would call hunting a sport. Although I am in no way opposed to hunting, isn't it interesting that what is sport to the hunter, is death to the prey?

It's a jungle out there

"Be sober, be vigilant; because your adversary the devil, as a roaring lion, walketh about, seeking whom he may devour…" (1 Peter 5:8).

The hunt is on; what kind of scent do you give off? You may be attracting predators.

As you romp through the jungle of love and relationships, is yours the scent of one who prays, or of one who is prey? Remember, the predator knows the difference — do you?

"For ye suffer, if a man bring you into bondage, if a man devour you, if a man take of you, if a man exalt himself, if a man smite you on the face" (2 Corinthians 11:20).

Removing the labels

"The Son of man is come eating and drinking; and ye say, Behold a gluttonous man, and a winebibber, a friend of publicans and sinners!" (Luke 7:34).

Labels come in many forms and are called by various names. The woman trying to reach the top of the corporate ladder with her dignity intact is labeled a 'B' because she demands respect, gives firm handshakes and doesn't show cleavage. The woman who studies hard and earns a degree while in prison is labeled an ex con. She finds that even with a degree, employers are reluctant to overlook the instructions on her label that say "do not hire". There are women with children who find dating next to impossible because even though they work everyday and are truly independent, they are labeled "Looking for a daddy". The fifty-something divorcee or widow is labeled "over the hill". Each label identifies a particular group of women and gives instructions on how to handle them. Labels ultimately force a woman to a point of decision in which she will either lower her standards or fight to maintain them. Labels become obstacles of fear and doubt that seem insurmountable. Whether given by society or self-inflicted, labels are always the source of the pitiful mark down process.

So where do these labels come from and how are they removed? Labels are the result of society's attempt to define who you are based on how you look, what you've done, where you are, and where you've been. A label accepted becomes the breaking of a woman's spirit. It is the dowsing of that fiery passion for the pursuit of her dreams. There is only one way to remove a label, and that is to reject it through *"Submit yourselves therefore to God. Resist the devil, and he will flee from you" (James 4:7)*. Let's do a comparison, who does how you look, what you've done, where you are and where you've been say that you are? Now, what does the Word say? Starting with how you look, the Bible says this: *"for the LORD seeth not as man seeth; for man looketh on the outward appearance, but the LORD looketh on the heart" (1 Samuel 16:7)*. As for what you've done, Romans 8:1 says, *"there is therefore now no condemnation to them which are in Christ Jesus, who walk not after the flesh, but after the Spirit."* What about where you are? Romans 5:3-5 says, *"And not only so, but we glory in tribulations also: knowing that tribulation worketh patience; And patience, xperience; and experience, hope: And hope makes us not ashamed; because the love of God is shed abroad in our hearts by the Holy Ghost which is given unto us."*

> Labels are the result of society's attempt to define who you are based on how you look, what you've done, where you are, and where you've been. A label accepted becomes the breaking of a woman's spirit.

Now, compare where you've been to Philippians 3: 13-14, "*I count not myself to have apprehended: but this one thing I do, forgetting those things which are behind, and reaching forth unto those things which are before, I press toward the mark for the prize of the high calling of God in Christ Jesus.*" You don't have to be hindered by the guilt of your past. You can praise God as you learn and grow where you are because you know that where you are is merely a stepping stone to your destiny! Finally, Romans 8:28 tells us that all things work together for good to them that love God, to them who are the called according to his purpose. Start applying God's word to your past and present and future and watch closely as He pulls your self esteem out of that bargain bin and places your standards back on the main showcase of life. You'll become a new creation defying every stereotype, surviving every rejection. No longer will bargain hunters in the church over use and under appreciateyour gifts. Bargain hunters at the office will be forced to pay you what you're worth. Your kindness and generosity will be viewed by those in relationship with you as strength and not weakness. I believe that as you're reading this book, the discount signs of desperation in the windows of your soul are being torn down! The Bible says that God opens a door and no man can close it! So from now on instead of asking why me, when opportunity knocks, begin to ask why not me! Why not give you the promotion? Why shouldn't a man of God love you? Why shouldn't your children respect and obey you? Col 1:12 says that God has qualified us to be partakers of the inheritance of the saints in the light. You're qualified, you're equipped, and God has put the tools you need to succeed inside of you. You just have to believe it! The moment you begin to believe that you are that designer's original, people will be forced to look at you for the virtuous woman that the word of God says that you are regardless of where you are now or have been in the past. Let society have their labels, but as for God's woman "there is neither Greek nor Jew, circumcision nor uncircumcision, Barbarian, Scythian, bond nor free: but Christ is all, and in all" (Colossians 3:11). Your very presence will command the respect given to all Proverbs 31:10 women. They are a rare and precious commodity whose price is far more than rubies! Through the grace of God and the truth of his word she overcomes every obstacle surpasses every expectation and removes every label.

You're still fab!

"A man that hath friends must show himself friendly."
(Proverbs 18:24).

F.A.B. is an acronym used in marketing meaning *Features Advantages and Benefits*. As I stated before, we all constantly marketing ourselves on some level or in some arena. Whenever you meet someone for the first time regardless of the setting you usually allow your marketing representative to do the talking. Your representative is given the task of presenting

you in the best possible light. She is who you would always be in a perfect world. It is not a perfect world however and the fact is like everyone else you're an imperfect person with your own set of issues, habits and quirks to deal with. Some might argue that using your representative is hypocritical but I disagree. Your representative is a part of you. She is who you aspire to be more consistently. You would be taken aback if someone approached you and said "Hi, my name is Marcus and I have a violent temper, pleased to meet you."

In verse nine, seeing no need to put her best foot forward, she immediately places her perceived inadequacies on display by citing that she is a Samaritan woman. Her race and gender must have been as obvious to Jesus as his was to her and so her brief monologue comes across as a bit of social satire and would be humorous were it not for sad fact that she means every word of it. An inherit sense of inferiority is truly at the core of this woman's beliefs. Progress is always brought to a screeching halt the moment we begin to see our issues as the sum of our life's equation. We must sell ourselves on the idea that we are more than what we have been through, and that we are better than where we are at the moment. Let's do a quick diagnostic; have you started dressing the way you feel instead of the way you know you can look? Have you begun to dread social events? Have you developed a fear of meeting new people? If you answered yes to all of these questions, chances are good that you've fired your representative. If you answered yes to one or two of these questions, your representative may only be laid off. May I suggest that it's time to make your way out any funk you may be in? Snap out of it, pat yourself on the back, get your hair done or spend a day at a spa. Put your representative back to work and allow her to say what God's word says about you, even when you don't believe it. You will in time, as faith comes by hearing the word of God (Romans 10:17). Remember that you're still F.A.B! There are features, advantages, and benefits for anyone fortunate enough to be in your circle!

You've got to accentuate the positive.
Eliminate the negative.
And latch on to the affirmative.

Don't mess with Mister In-Between.
You've got to spread joy up to the maximum.
Bring gloom down to the minimum.
Have faith or pandemonium's.
Liable to walk upon the scene.

- By Johnny Mercer & Harold Arlen

Timing Isn't Everything

"So, why me?" the woman wonders. The answer is simple. Why not her? She is completely equipped to give Jesus a drink. She has the tools, the knowledge, the experience and the resources. She is in the right place at the right time. The problem is that she has the wrong mind! This woman's ability is totally useless because her mind is held captive. Remember that your gifting, your talents and every wonderful thing you have to offer will always be chained behind the wall of your insecurities. Captivity always starts in the mind but will manifest itself through actions. That is why some women who are victims of sexual abuse as children often develop problems with intimacy or throw themselves headlong into promiscuity as adults. Although many go on to have successful careers, and marry, raise children, pastor churches and live life as mature adults. It is in

> Remember that your gifting, your talents and every wonderful thing you have to offer will always be chained behind the wall of your insecurities.

the realm of Intimacy in which time for them has been warped as they remain defenseless little girls alone in the darkened rooms of a past incident.

Terrified and unable to trust; they fail to recognize seasons and opportunities to be healed and made whole. You must understand that *"God has not given you the spirit of fear, but of a power, love, and of a sound mind" (2 Timothy 1:7).*

Is your past affecting your present and hindering your future?

You may already be in the right place at the right time. The question is, where is your mind?

Her Worldview

ABC'S & 123'S

"...Sir, You have nothing to draw with, and the well is deep. Where then do You get that living water? Are You greater than our father Jacob, who gave us the well, and drank from it himself, as well as his sons and his livestock?" (John 4:11-12, NKJV).

How we see the world ultimately emanates from how we see ourselves. This woman's view of the world is through a cloudy lens of low self esteem. After hearing Jesus' offer to give her living water, she attempts in verse 11 to superimpose her own doubts and fears on to Him. She tells Jesus that the well is deep and he has nothing to draw water with. She wonders where he will get this water. "Are you greater than my father Jacob who built this well she asked?" In other words,

> How we see the world ultimately emanates from how we see ourselves.

A. It's out of your reach

B. You don't have the resources

C. You can't surpass those who came before you

These are the same limitations that have hindered her own life's progress. I call them the ABC's of self destruction. These three life destroying statements are the most frequently given reasons that people cite for you to cease from pursuing your dreams. Misery indeed loves company and is very contagious. Also understand these three principles:

1.   Hurting people hurt people.

2.   Hindered people hinder people

3.   Defeated people defeat people

These are the 123's of self preservation. People in these states are dangerous. They are naturally drawn to what they are or will attempt to change people and environments to fit their own negative view of the world. One hard reality of life is that you may have friends, family, co-workers and even members of your church family who can't, or won't see you succeeding where others have failed. If allowed, they will sow seeds of fear and doubt that will become a harvest of self destruction in your life. These seeds of negativity if not cut off at the root, will continue to produce and create generations of underachievers. "This I say therefore, and testify in the Lord, that ye henceforth walk not as other Gentiles walk, in the vanity of their mind, Having the understanding darkened, being alienated from the life of God through the ignorance that is in them, because of the blindness of their heart"

(Ephesians 4:17-18). Jesus came to give you give you anabundant life (John 10:10) be mindful not to let anyone steal that life from you.

Just Answer the Question

"But whom say ye that I am?" (Matthew 16:15b).

Isn't it incredible that a question asked 2,000 years ago still demands an answer, still challenges us today? This question, if answered correctly, will radically alter the direction of your life and set you on a course to achieving your dreams. This is the key to unlocking every door that has ever been closed in your face! Do you know who Jesus is and that he has plans to prosper you and to see you succeed where others have failed?

In Matthew 16: 13 the disciples are explaining to Jesus that there are many opinions circulating in reference to who he is. As with the woman there are labels being suggested to determine his status. *"And they said, Some say that thou art John the Baptist: some, Elias; and others, Jeremias, or one of the prophets" (Matthew 16:14).* None of these labels taken at face value are negative. However, to assign any one of them to Jesus would put Him in a box and take away the part of him that is from God, and yet is God. If accepted, these labels would put limitations on him and hinder his movement toward purpose and destiny. Jesus needs to be put to death on a cross as a sinless sacrifice. *"For he hath made him to be sin for us, who knew no sin; that we might be made the righteousness of God in him" (2 Corinthians 5:21).* This feat cannot not be accomplished if he is merely a prophet no matter how revered; or a baptist no matter how great. In order to accomplish this mission; Jesus needs to be who and what he was born to be. After finding out what others are saying, he asks his disciples the life changing question, *"He saith unto them, 'But whom say ye that I am?'* And Simon Peter answered and said, *'Thou art the Christ, the Son of the living God'* (Matthew 16:16).* Jesus then explains that flesh and blood could not have given Peter the answer. Like the woman with her jaded world view you will find that because of the limited scope of human foresight people often require a reference point for your ambitions, or they may need someone to compare you to. In most cases, those closest to us are either unwilling or unable to comprehend true originality. They don't understand that you are destined to do something that has not been done before. Throughout history, those who are truly innovative in their thinking and radical in their ambitions have been initially dismissed and considered crazy. But don't you be discouraged; time and success will vindicate you. The very people who discarded you will one day honor you. However, while you're praising God for your future triumphs, let's not forget that present obstacles require your immediate focus, and the lack of current support is demanding your absolute tenacity.

In dealing with support, or the lack thereof, I do not want to vilify your friends and loved ones. They may not be malicious in their failure to cheer you on, some simply do not understand that the goals you have set for your life are not out of reach, or that like the woman you have already been given the necessary tools. *"Moreover whom he did predestinate, them he also called: and whom he called, them he also justified: and whom he justified, them he also glorified" (Romans 8:30).* You have been predestined for greatness, called to uniqueness, and the mistakes you've made along the way have been justified as part the necessary process. Knowing who Jesus is will enable you to do far greater than all those who came before you!

"Verily, verily, I say unto verily, I say unto you, He that believeth on me, the works that I do shall he do also; and greater works than these shall he do; because I go unto my Father" (John 14:12). From that very moment of divine enlightenment, Simon's name was changed to Peter, meaning 'Rock', and his destiny was forever altered. In Matthew 16:18 Jesus declares that Peter's revelation of Him would be the foundation upon which his ultimate purpose and kingdom would be built. Because Peter answered correctly, Jesus gave him the keys to that kingdom! The Bible says that people perish from a lack of knowledge. Therefore the opposite must also be true. An abundance of knowledge and revelation of who Jesus is will cause you to live and prosper. As with Peter's revelation of Jesus, understand that when you are in the company of

people who truly know the answer to the question, they will not doubt what you are capable of through Christ. "*I can do all things through Christ which strengtheneth me*" (Philippians 4:13). This is the rock upon which you can begin unhindered to build your dream life!

Who died and left you in charge?

"That being justified by his grace, we should be made heirs according to the hope of eternal life." (Titus 3:7).

The slave surveys the master's estate and wishes she could have it. The heir, however, sees the same estate, but knowing who she is connected to proclaims, "my father has already prepared it for me!"

You have not because you ask not; perhaps you haven't asked because you don't know.

Perhaps it is time to stop living the life of a slave on an estate that has been freely given to you.

In verse ten of the text Jesus explains to the woman that she doesn't know who he is or else she would ask and He would give her living water. What if you had a very wealthy relative who died and left you a multi-million dollar estate, but you were not notified? What if you were never told of your connection to someone of great resource, power, and influence? True, one cannot miss what one has never had, but you will have most certainly missed out on what is rightfully yours. *"Now we have received, not the spirit of the world, but the spirit which is of God; that we might know the things that are*

Knowing who you are

Knowing who you are and who you're connected to changes your thought life and conversation. There is an exodus that must take place from the bondage of wishful thinking and the accepting of handouts. One must be led by the Word to the freedom of asking, believing, and receiving. Do not simply accept any and everything thrown your way, but question everything. Is this who you really are? Is that all life has to offer? You already now who people say that you are, but now begin to ask the Lord; "who do you say that I am?" Your world view will change the moment He speaks the life changing answer and tells you exactly who you are. Don't be alarmed, his answer may not be based on anything visible to you at the time; in fact you may be the exact opposite of who and what he proclaims. *"...even God, who quickeneth the dead, and calleth those things which be not as though they were" (Romans 4:17)*. Allow God to quicken the dreams in your life that are dead and repair every broken ambition. You must nderstand that God sees you far beyond your current state. Overlooking your present condition, He calls you what you are not as though you were all along. Going forward, begin to see yourself and the world through the eyes of Christ and your decisions in life will be made not from a place of desperation but divine inspiration! Isn't it awesome to know that God has enabled you to go where no one said you could, that you've been empowered to do what everyone said could not be done? Make the decision today to stop allowing people, circumstances and especially the voice of past mistakes tell you that the well of your dreams is too deep, and that you have nothing to draw with. You don't have to be held back any longer. You may have lost some years, but it's not too late. God is a restorer of years (Joel 2:25). You may be in the last chapter of your life but it can still be the greatest chapter! By the grace and favor of God, there is still time for you to make an impact! There is still time to make every remaining moment of your life count!

Allow God to quicken the dreams in your life that are dead and repair every broken ambition. You must understand that God sees you far beyond your current state. Overlooking your present condition, He calls you what you are not as though you were all along.

For I know the thoughts that I think toward you, saith the LORD, thoughts of peace, and not of evil, to give you an expected end" (Jeremiah 29:11). There is a definite sense of relief in knowing that God has a method to what seems to be the madness of life. One finds peace in realizing that God has declared the end from the beginning! Even in the most trying times of your life, when it seemed the entire universe had conspired against you, God was on your side whether you knew it or not. He bottled up every tear and felt every pain. He has promised that everyone who sows in tears will reap a harvest of joy! So it's not where you start that matters most, but where you end. So know, and start speaking aloud that you are a winner. The same promise that Jesus gave to Peter is given to you as well. The gates of hell will not prevail! Knowing Jesus will give birth to that greater understanding of who he is in you and who you are in him.

Supply and Demand

> *"She perceiveth that her merchandise is good: her candle goeth not out by night"* (Proverbs 31:18).

Supply and demand is perhaps the most fundamental concept in economics and is the backbone of an open market. Demand refers to how much of a product or service is desired. Supply represents how much of that product one has to offer. If the demand is greater than the supply, the product becomes valuable. If the supply becomes greater than demand, it loses value.

Rahab in the second chapter of the book of Joshua is a wonderful illustration of supply and demand as it relates to you as a woman. Rahab is a single woman working as a prostitute in the city of Jericho. The Israelite army is going to invade soon, and Jericho's days are numbered. The entire city is shaking and the heart of every citizen has failed for fear of the Israelite army. Rahab, however, has a uniquely different world view than those around her. As the two spies enter her house, She should be frightened out of her wits like everyone else but instead, she sees their coming not as an end, but as the possibility of a new beginning. Rahab is in the right place at the right time; with the right mind. In contrast to the Samaritan woman, Rahab does not allow her current social status to override the fact that she has something to offer. The invasion would crush Jericho physically and economically. Still, she realizes that she has in her possession something these two men cannot get anywhere else. Rahab understands supply and demand. The spies are in desperate need of a hiding place, and she alone can offer them one. This will not be a hand out and she is not asking for welfare. This is an exchange. *"And the men answered her, our life for yours, if ye utter not this business. And it shall be, when the LORD hath given us the land that we will deal kindly and truly with thee"* (Joshua 2:14). Her life, hopes, and dreams are equally important in this relationship. Realize that you are a valuable part of any relationship, be it business or personal. You don't have to put your life or

Never camouflage the uniqueness of who you are or what you have, for fear of criticism. Find your market niche and work it.

dreams on a shelf for anyone. I believe that it is her knowledge of what she is bringing to the negotiating table that gives Rahab the courage she needs to overcome her fear and ask for the position. She knows that the demand for a hiding place is high, and that the supply is low. As a result, she is able to corner the market by distinguishing herself from those around her. She becomes a one woman monopoly, leaving the spies no choice but to hire her. As a result, she is able to quit the prostitution business and be introduced and accepted into the inner circle of the most blessed and powerful community on the face of the planet! Till this day she is named in the direct bloodline of Jesus Christ, a position that based on her label she should have never been qualified for! "And Joshua saved Rahab the harlot alive, and her father's household, and all that she had; and she dwelleth in Israel even unto this day; because she hid the messengers, which Joshua sent to spy out Jericho" (Joshua 6:25). Understand that always striving to fit into your surroundings can be detrimental to your growth. Never camouflage the uniqueness of who you are or what you have, for fear of criticism. Find your market niche and work it. Understand that when you become like everyone else, the supply becomes greater than demand and you lose value. Therefore corner the market in everything that is uniquely you. *"Now therefore, if ye will obey my voice indeed, and keep my covenant, then ye shall be a peculiar treasure unto me above all people: for all the earth is mine" (Exodus 19:5).* Your gifts are designed to make room for you. Allow God to use those gifts to create a demand for what you alone can supply and you will go far. *"Ye are the light of the world. A city that is set on an hill cannot be hid" (Matthew 5:14).* The moment you perceive that your merchandise is good, no one will be able to put your candle out and you will see the world as a puzzle needing one crucial piece for completion…you!

Daddy's little girls

"Even as Sara obeyed Abraham, calling him lord: whose daughters ye are, as long as ye do well, and are not afraid with any amazement" (1 Peter 3:6).

In Genesis 12:3 God made Abraham a promise that through him, all families would be blessed. Even after Abraham is laid to rest, the blessing would be passed on continually as an inheritance, thereby making us all Abraham's seed. However, as rule of thumb, the right to claim this inheritance belonged to the first born male child of each family. This birth right was to be passed from father to son to ensure proper distribution for generations to come. It must have been difficult being a daughter in ancient times. The source of a father's pride was in the birth of many sons. Usually, daughters are not even included in the biblical numbering of a man's children. Here however, God, who has no respect of persons, clearly reminds you that as daughters, you are also heirs to this promise. He does, however, clearly state that your entitlement to the inheritance is conditional. Without pretense God requires that daughters who are to be heirs must do well and be fearless. Ask any woman who has achieved any measure of success in a male dominated environment and she will testify to you that without maintaining these two standards, she would not have accomplished anything. I believe this passage of Scripture is prophetic in that God knew that you would have to play on an unleveled playing field. He understood that his daughters then and now would have to be twice as good as their male counterparts to be considered half as bad. He knew that being the only skirt in a lobby full of pinstriped suits and wing-tipped shoes awaiting an interview could be frightening. God in his infinite wisdom also understood that someday his daughters would have to have to play on an unleveled playing field. He understood that his daughters then and now would have to be twice as good as their male counterparts to be considered half as bad. He knew that being the only skirt in a lobby full of

pinstriped suits and wing-tipped shoes awaiting an interview could be frightening. God in his infinite wisdom also understood that someday his daughters would have to stare into the stoic faces of male board members to give presentations and make proposals without flinching. Do well, and be fearless; these stipulations are not loop holes or escape clauses in an otherwise binding agreement; neither are they designed to undermine your success. Instead, they were written into the agreement to challenge you as daughters to become go-getters who will not wait for their dreams to be handed to them. The five daughters of Zelophehad in the 27th chapter of the book of Numbers are a prime example of women who decided to break the rule of thumb, and climb over the social, religious and economic barricades to gain the equality that was rightfully theirs. Mahlah, Noah, and Hoglah, and Milcah, and Tirzah whose names mean, in the same order, sickness, consolation, festive, queen, and benevolent. Though their names indicated very different personalities, they were united by a common goal. *"And they stood before Moses, and before Eleazar the priest, and before the princes and all the congregation, by the door of the tabernacle of the congregation, saying, "Our father died in the wilderness, and he was not in the company of them that gathered themselves together against the LORD in the company of Korah; but died in his own sin, and had no sons. Why should the name of our father be done away from among his family, because he hath no son? Give unto us therefore a possession among the brethren of our father"* (Numbers 27:2-4). Imagine the courage it must have taken to stand before Moses, along with a host of both priest and

> There were undoubtedly those who tried to talk them out of what must have seemed like an utterly absurd idea. These women however, were radical in faith, and relentless in the pursuit of their inheritance.

prince alike and give such a daring proposal. The planning would have to be precise. Unlike their male counterparts, they would be given no margin for error. They did not interact with these men of stature in social functions. They did not have a chance to sell their idea informally on a golf course or in a steam room. They would have this one chance to make it happen, and it would have to be done well, and without fear. Merely obtaining an audience may have been a feat within itself. They would have to work seamlessly together with each daughter's personality bringing something unique to the team. They would undoubtedly need Milcah, meaning queen, for leadership. Tirzah the benevolent one would be given the task of shaking the right hands and establishing rapport with key people who could open doors for them. Hoglah the festive one would bring balance, so as not to allow her sisters to be consumed by their work and forget to let
their hair down and live a little. Though Mahlah may have been sickly and therefore not as strong as her sisters, she would have Noah, as a source of consolation and who understood that the strong ought to bear the infirmities of the weak (Romans 15:1). If these five daughters had been born sons, there would not have been an issue to begin with, but instead, The bar was raised higher for Zelophehad's daughters than for the average male. Certainly there were those men and women alike who expected them to fail. There were undoubtedly those who tried to talk them out of what must have seemed like an utterly absurd idea. These women however, were radical in faith, and relentless in the pursuit of their

inheritance.

- I can do all things through Christ which strengthens me *(Philippians 4:13)*.

- Trust in the LORD, and do good; so shalt thou dwell in the land, and verily thou shalt be fed *(Psalms 37:3)*.

- The LORD is my light and my salvation; whom shall I fear? The LORD is the strength of my life; of whom shall I be afraid? *(Psalms 27:1)*.

Either your fears will cancel your faith, or your faith will cancel your fears. The moment you begin to lose faith in what you are called to do, you lose the drive to do it well.

Allow these three scriptures to become your heart's mantra and they will cause your faith to make you fearless and you will do with excellence and perseverance whatever you set your mind to do. *"And Moses brought their cause before the LORD. And the LORD spake unto Moses, saying, The daughters of Zelophehad speak right: thou shalt surely give them a possession of an inheritance among their father's brethren; and thou shalt cause the inheritance of their father to pass unto them And thou shalt speak unto the children of Israel, saying, If a man die, and have no son, then ye shall cause his inheritance to pass unto his daughter"* (Numbers 27:5-8).

The daughters' presentation must have been so eloquent, and their argument so convincing that Moses had to take their case to God. Not only did God agree with Zelophehad's daughters, he made a decree that would bless other women who would otherwise be denied an inheritance based on gender alone. Their spirit of excellence and fearlessness prevailed and a new precedent was set. The message of their victory still reverberates in our ears today. No matter how unleveled the playing field is, even in the face of double standards and chauvinistic mentalities you can still succeed! The God of Abraham Isaac and Jacob is no respecter of persons. Daddy's little girls are heirs to the promise too!

Women believe me!

> *"Jesus saith unto her, Woman, believe me, the hour cometh, when ye shall neither in this mountain, nor yet at Jerusalem, worship the Father" (John 4:21).*

In order for God's perfect will to be accomplished in your life, you will need to go back to the basics of who you are. In Biblical times, a person's name was often a reflection of the parents' opinion of the child or of their future expectations. At times a name could even be a reminder of unpleasant circumstances. The name Mary, for instance, means bitterness; or Jabez, his name was a reminder of the great pain his mother endured while giving birth to him (*1 Chronicles 4:9*). It is therefore noteworthy that Jesus never bothers to ask the woman her name. Perhaps her birth name was a reminder of someone's pain or disapproval. Instead Jesus takes her back to Eden; back to her moment of creation. *"And so it is written, the first man Adam was made a living soul; the last Adam was made a quickening spirit" (1 Corinthians 15:45).* Here, we witness a moment of déjà vu as Jesus, the last Adam, looks on God's work of art just as the first Adam looked on Eve and calls her what she truly is: Woman! He then tells her to believe him. Jesus wants her to believe that a change is coming. God will never assign you a task without giving you the ability to perform it. Therefore when he tells you to believe, He is fully aware that your faith has taken a pounding. After so much heartache and disappointment, your faith may not be where it once was, and your ability to persevere is quite possibly not what it used to be. Simply put, you're exhausted. God has to therefore take you back to Eden in your spirit and give you another moment of creation. *"Therefore if any man be in Christ, he is a new creature: old things are passed away; behold, all things are become new" (2 Corinthians 5:17)*. In your original moment of creation, no one has hurt you. Your heart has not been broken and life holds no disappointments — only endless possibilities. There are no memories of abuse to contend with in your mind. No feelings of bitterness fighting for space in your heart. In your creation moment, you are at peace with God and you are comfortable in your own skin. Your view of the world is not jaded and you allow yourself to love and be loved, to trust and be trusted. *"Love suffereth long, and is kind; Love envieth not; Love vaunteth not itself, is not puffed up, Doth not behave itself unseemly, seeketh not her own, is not easily provoked, thinketh no evil; Rejoiceth not in iniquity, but rejoiceth in the truth; Beareth all things, believeth all things, hopeth all things, endureth all things" (1 Corinthians 13: 4-7)*. The

> In your creation moment, you are at peace with God and you are comfortable in your own skin. Your view of the world is not jaded and you allow yourself to love and be loved, to trust and be trusted.

woman believes that this kind of love life will be possible when the Messiah comes along someday; but Jesus informs her that she is talking to the Messiah (*John 4:26*)! "*Jesus said unto her, I am the resurrection, and the life: he that believeth in me, though he were dead, yet shall he live*" (*John 11:25*). Jesus wants to revive every dead place in your life. He wants you to rediscover your stride. Allow him to give you a well deserved make over. Let him add a touch of class and restore that hint of sass that you've lost. The poet Lorenzo wrote this refrain: "*You have braved the times of change and preserved through the malice of men You were once highly respected you shall soon be again*". Your moment is coming and now is. Woman believe me!

Her Relationships

Oh Well; You've got your reasons

"The woman said to Him, Sir, give me this water, that I may not thirst, nor come here to draw." (John 4:15).

Who this woman is connected to has been taught and preached at length, but in dealing with her relationships this time, let's first examine what she was connected to. In verse 15, her self esteem takes an upward turn, triggering an adjustment to her world view. She begins to see that Jesus will not be hindered by the voice of her limitations. Like Rahab, this woman senses that this is not some haphazard event. She must be valuable. Why else would Jesus break down the social, economical, and religious barriers that separated Samaritans from Jews for so long? I believe she realized that Destiny was staring her in the face and might not ever do so again. Notice that in verse 15 her conversation is also changing. The water she once thought was impossible to obtain, she now believes is hers for the asking! *"Sir, give me this water that I may not thirst, nor come here to draw" (John 4:15b).*

Remember, Jesus told the woman if she knew she would ask. There may have been a myriad of reasons for wanting this living water Jesus offered. However, only two were discussed. First, that she would never thirst again, which is indicative of her desire for salvation and righteousness. *"Blessed are they which do hunger and thirst after righteousness: for they shall be filled" (Matthew 5:6).* Then, there was her second reason, which I believe holds the key to living life to the fullest. Though grossly overlooked, the weight of the entire text rests on the foundation of this one line: "*…neither come here to draw.*" She wanted to be disconnected from the well. It is this woman's relationship to an inanimate object that is keeping her bound more so than any man ever could.

In order to understand why disconnection from the well is more important to her than leaving the man she is with, you must first understand some facts about wells. Wells provide water in places where there was no above ground water. In ancient times, wherever a fresh water source was found a well would be dug, and a community would be built around it. Her ancestor Jacob established himself in proximity to this well because without it there could be no thriving community. It is important to understand that the well was the center of her world. Everyone she knew, everyone she loved, everything she had, was connected to and dependant upon this well for existence. In essence, she was asking for a way out of the system. She wanted to break the cycle of dependency in her life. Generations of her family and friends had all been dependant upon this well to sustain themselves! What I'm going to say next will upset some, will enlighten others and will undoubtedly challenge the traditionalist point of view…salvation is not enough. Now, before you throw this book in the nearest trash can shouting "the devil is a liar," please hear me out. 3 John 1:2 says, *"Beloved, I wish above all things that thou mayest prosper and be in health, even as thy soul prospereth"*. You and I have been saved by grace from the penalty of sin. Jesus was the perfect sacrifice, the lamb that was slain before the foundation of the world. He took on the guilt of sin through the suffering of the cross. I struggle to contain myself even now as I write. For what can wash away my sins? Nothing but the blood of Jesus. What can make me whole again…but wait, how many blood washed people remain unfulfilled in other areas of life? Why are so many saved people lonely and depressed? How many Christians live year after year in debt? How many tongue talking, Bible-thumping people do you know who are not seeing their dreams become reality? Sure, they all love God and there is a place prepared for them in heaven, but what about this life? "Thy kingdom come, Thy will be done in earth as it is in heaven" (Matthew 6:10). This woman wanted more out of life. Far too many Christians settle for a one dimensional life. To condense Christianity to the Sunday morning experience alone is to rob yourself of the abundant life you are meant to have in Christ. What she now wants is to prosper and be in health just as her soul is about to prosper. She is after all,

> Spiritual, physical, and financial prosperity, true wholeness and true holiness are found when these three are working as one in the life of the believer.

living in a three dimensional world, dealing with a three dimensional struggle, why not have a three dimensional life transformation? Spiritual, physical, and financial prosperity, true wholeness and true holiness are found when these three are working as one in the life of the believer. Do not settle for salvation from sin alone, but seek salvation from poverty and dysfunctional relationships as well. This woman wants to be free from every shackle in her life. She wants to remove the labels that keep her in a perpetual state of wondering if there is life beyond the well, or outside of her small town. Perhaps she wants salvation from wondering if she can ever be something more than a Samaritan woman. "*But as it is written, Eye hath not seen, nor ear heard, neither have entered into the heart of man, the things which God hath prepared for them that love him*" (1 Corinthians 2:9).

Understand that Jesus is not only a savior to those who seek him; he is also a rewarder (*Hebrews 11:6*). Those closest to you may not understand your longing. They may even ask why, but you don't have to explain anything. Just tell them you've got your reasons. Jesus is waiting to hear them all!

Who's filling you?

"...but they mingled among the heathen and learned their works" (Psalms 106:35).

True, this woman has been married five times and is now involved with a man who is not her own. Jesus, however, does not dwell on the issue, so I won't either. He commends her on her honesty and it is important that we honestly assess our strengths and weaknesses. The Word of God tells us to examine our ways and test them (*2 Corinthians 13:5*). In examining one's ways one will find without  exception that his ways, good and bad, are due in large part to past and present environments. From childhood to this very moment, everyone connected to you has been or currently is a well. This means that whether indirectly, by example, or by direct instruction you've been drawing from them. Over the years you have reached into various wells to draw essential life lessons pertaining to love, sex, money, education, religion, and more. The problem is some wells from which you draw or have drawn are contaminated. This woman like many others had been drinking non potable life lessons that were slowly poisoning her, and stunting her growth. These poisoned wells would have a crippling effect over time on many levels. Did you learn about marriage from divorced people? Did you learn most of what you know about men from other women? Were you taught how to pay bills by people with bad credit and no savings? It's important that you begin to surround yourself with people from whom you can draw life, wisdom, and solid instruction. To some degree, we have all been victims of a poisoned mis-education, but now we must allow God to detoxify our minds. *"And be renewed in the spirit of your mind" (Ephesians 4:23).*

> From childhood to this very moment, everyone connected to you has been or currently is a well. This means that whether indirectly, by example, or by direct instruction you've been drawing from them.

Family matters?

"While he yet talked to the people, behold, his mother and his brethren stood without, desiring to speak with him. Then one said unto him, Behold, thy mother and thy brethren stand without, desiring to speak with thee But he answered and said unto him that told him, Who is my mother? And who are my brethren? And he stretched forth his hand toward his disciples, and said, behold my mother and my brethren! For whosoever shall do the will of my Father which is in heaven, the same is my brother, and sister, and mother"
Matthew 12:46-50).

God wants to hook you up! There are people with whom your path has not yet crossed, who have been predestined to sow into your life. *"And the Lord said unto him, Arise, and go into the street which is called Straight, and enquire in the house of Judas for one called Saul, of Tarsus: for, behold, he prayeth, And hath seen in a vision a man named Ananias coming in, and putting his hand on him, that he might receive his sight"* (Acts 9: 1-12). These sowers will not be relatives. They will be on direct assignment from God to push you toward your purpose! God wants to connect you to people who will bring out the best in you and challenge you to improve what is worst in you! These will be people who agree that you are someone special. They will understand that you are a woman of distinct purpose and destiny. Those who do not agree should not be allowed to walk with you. Does this mean that you are to cut all ties with everyone around you? That you can't go to the family reunion or the Labor Day cook out? That's not what I'm saying at all. I am saying that when the Bible speaks of two walking together, it is referring to close relationship, more so than casual acquaintances. You can certainly catch a movie with someone without integrating that person into your life plan. There are some, however, whose situations require more drastic measures. When Jesus came home to Nazareth for a visit, instead of giving him the welcome due a hometown hero, they booed him and were unwilling to accept that someone from the 'hood had become something wonderful in life. Their unbelief and disdain for his growth and success limited his ability to do miracles there. "And they were offended in him. But Jesus said unto them, A prophet is not without honor, save in

> The truth is, there are those who will never see you the way God sees you. Ultimately you will need to decide the extent of the severing that is needed in your life.

his own country, and in his own house And he did not many mighty works there because of their unbelief" (Matthew 13:57-58). The truth is, there are those who will never see you the way God sees you. Ultimately you will need to decide the extent of the severing that is needed in your life. I recommend that you hear God, trust his wisdom, and obey his commandment knowing that anyone or anything you give up for God will pale in comparison to what you receive from God for your obedience!

"And every one that hath forsaken houses, or brethren, or sisters, or father, or mother, or wife, or children, or lands, for my name's sake, shall receive an hundredfold, and shall inherit everlasting life" (Matthew 19:29).

Check your crowd

"Blessed is the man that walketh not in the counsel of the ungodly, nor standeth in the way of sinners, nor sitteth in the seat of the scornful" (Psalm 1:1).

The Bible says that two cannot walk together except they are in agreement (Amos 3:3). The question must now be asked, on what do we agree? Understand that it is just as easy to agree on failure as it is to agree on success. Check your crowd. Are your friends happy about your promotion; are they slow to applaud your weight loss, but quick to point out your gain? Do your friends find fault with every man you date?

Careful, you may be walking in the council of the ungodly or sitting in the seat of scornful, negative individuals. This woman is to her own detriment – walking in complete agreement with people who share her low self-esteem and negative worldview. Take a look at the woman with the issue of blood (*Mark 5:25*). She was in the right crowd. In biblical times, a woman was considered unclean during her cycle; consequently, anyone who touched her would also be considered unclean. As she crawled after Jesus to touch his garment the crowd should have parted as people tried to get away from her. This, however, did not happen; instead she had to crawl through the crowd. *"When she had heard of Jesus, she came in the press behind, and touched his garment" (Mark 5:27).* The reason there was such a press was that these of people were far too busy trying to get to Jesus for their own reasons to be critical of anyone else! The point being: if you're the only crab fighting to get out of the pot, you're in the wrong crowd.

Exit Stage Right

"A time to weep, and a time to laugh; a time to mourn, and a time to dance" (Ecclesiastes 3:4).

In the third chapter of Ecclesiastes, Solomon teaches us there is a time for every purpose. Time then becomes the stage upon which God's purpose plays out in one's life. Problems arise when we fail to exit one stage or enter another. Some characters must exit the stage so that others may enter and the storyline can advance as planned. Ask yourself, how is this relationship advancing the story at this stage of your life? Is your ongoing dialogue with a particular character serving God's purpose, or are you prolonging a scene that should have ended by now? Let's go over your lines again.

You: "*Thou hast turned for me my mourning into dancing: thou hast put off my sackcloth, and girded me with gladness*" *(Psalms 30:11)*. Your crying scene has ended and according to the script, you should be dancing!

You've Got Mail

Imagine for a moment that you could not feel pain of any kind. Wouldn't that be a wonderful way to live? What genius ever thought of pain in the first place? Let's pretend that you have been granted this dream life in which pain does not exist. A few days into your blissful experience you notice that your pinky finger is the size of your big toe, and is turning green. You can't imagine what could possibly be wrong. Did you smash it while hanging that picture the other day? Under normal circumstances there would be no struggle to recall something as painfully obvious as a hammer thundering

Pain is often the first indicator that something is wrong. However, some women make the mistake of ignoring the pain until it is no longer felt.

down on your delicate well-manicured finger, but remember—you no longer feel pain. Should you apply ice, or is heat the answer? How can you effectively treat what you cannot diagnose? Finally, after every home remedy has failed and the condition of your finger has worsened, you relent to see a doctor. Once in the doctor's office, the doctor informs you that you have an infection caused by a splinter. You begin to wonder how the affects of a little splinter have grown so far out of proportion. The doctor explains that in most cases a splinter is fairly obvious. You feel pain and a sense that a foreign body is embedded in the skin. He tells you that by not getting treated sooner, you have compounded your problems. He cannot remove the splinter until he can bring the infection under control. Worst case scenario; he might have to amputate. You gasp at the thought of losing your finger. How did it go this far? Why didn't anyone notice; why didn't some one say something? All these questions bombard your mind and the answer becomes painfully obvious. You've lost something. What you thought was a gift is becoming a disaster. You realize that you needed your pain. If only you could have felt that slight pain early on, you would have taken steps to remedy the situation. God is indeed all-knowing. He is infinite in his wisdom and love toward us in that he gave us all the ability to feel pain as a defense both physically, emotionally and yes, even spiritually. "I Daniel was grieved in my spirit in the midst of my body, and the visions of my head troubled me" (Daniel 7:15). We know pleasure only in contrast to pain. Love becomes real when we are acquainted with the reality of hate. The joy of the father's acceptance of us through Christ, in all our wretchedness can only be fully appreciated or understood when placed against the backdrop of Jesus' painful rejection at Calvary. "He is despised and rejected of men; a man of sorrows, and acquainted with grief: and we hid as it were our faces from him; he was despised, and we esteemed him not" (Isaiah 53:3).

Please don't misinterpret what I am saying. Pain should not be desired, but it is necessary. Not to define you, but to alert you.

Therefore, don't ignore the pain you feel when you're being mistreated. Pain is often the first indicator that something is wrong. However, some women make the mistake of ignoring the pain until it is no longer felt. Much like the Samaritan woman, these women fluctuate from one relationship to another, attempting to survive in a volatile market by numbing themselves. All humans have physical nerve endings, but did you know that you have also been equipped with spiritual and emotional nerve endings as well? Nerve endings have receptors that send your brain messages causing you to respond to touch, vibration, pressure, cold, and warmth. Other nerve endings are equipped with nociceptors (no-sih-SEP-turs) —which are receptors that detect actual or potential damage. Nociceptors are most concentrated in areas that are more prone to injury, such as your fingers and toes. Sensations of severe pain are messaged almost instantaneously. I believe that God created us with spiritual and emotional nociceptors responding not only to damage but to potential damage in the areas of our lives that are most vulnerable. The heart, the mind, and the soul are all more susceptible to damage. These are the easiest to hurt and the most difficult to heal. Given a few weeks and you will use that finger again, but a broken heart a wounded soul or a tormented mind could last the rest of your life. Time does not heal all wounds; that's why it is imperative that we give these vulnerable areas to God first. *"Jesus said unto him, Thou shalt love the Lord thy God with all thy heart, and with all thy soul, and with all thy mind" (Matthew 22:37)*. The moment you give your heart, soul, and mind to God, He will stand and guard the gates of your self-esteem. He will also be a fence around your prayer life, your worship, your joy, and your survival instincts, making them restricted areas. You will then be able to allow yourself to love and be loved knowing that you are giving 100% of what God has allotted to the people you love.

If you are being hurt in your spirit or your emotions, check your inbox. The message has been sent with high priority. You need only respond and make the necessary adjustments. Pain is that messenger. Therefore building up a tolerance to it will not minimize the damage; it will only slow your response time. Years have been lost and lives destroyed because of slow responses to pain. Too many women have made the mistake of staying too long in abusive relationships, tolerating pain in exchange for help with bills or other perceived benefits. Understand that big houses and luxury cars, fine jewelry and gourmet food are not worth one's emotional or physical well being. *"Better is a dry morsel and quietness therewith, than a house full of sacrifices with strife"* (Proverbs 17:1). Also understand that abuse is not limited to striking or malicious language. The word abuse is derived from the words abnormal and use. Any type of abnormal use can be considered abusive. Abnormal use of your time and talent may be taking place on your job or in your church or in your friendships. Pain pushes you to survive by motivating you to move away from its source. Some women use excuses as pain killers—e.g. *"He's been under a lot of pressure lately,"* or *"They don't mean any harm.*" Pain killers are not a cure for what's causing the pain; they are designed to dull your sensitivity to it. Read the label of any pain medicine and it will advise you to consult a physician when symptoms persist as this may be the result of a more serious illness. The problem with numbing an area that is hurting is that numbing not only takes away pain, it takes away the ability to feel all together. As a result, a woman may find herself existing in an emotional vacuum without pain or pleasure, sorrow or joy. Make sure you're delivered, and not just numb. If you're no longer hurting and yet you're still not happy, you have probably over-medicated a more serious illness within a particular relationship. The symptoms have not gone away, you're just not feeling them anymore. My prayer is that after reading this book you will respond to your God-given instant messaging system and remind yourself that you deserve more. You've been numb too long. Your friends and loved ones can see when you are hurting. Still, if the truth were to ever be told, the symptoms that people see, like this woman's five failed marriages, for example, are nothing compared to the symptoms you have probably managed to keep hidden. Try as they may to advise you, and for all their pleading, you have continued to anestisize yourself with pain killers. A desire for complete healing and deliverance must come from an inward response by way of an outward cry to the Father. Perhaps you have been numb so long that you have become fearful. You're afraid that a response at this point in your life would mean being overwhelmed by your pain or drowned by your tears. After all, you've got a business to run, or children to raise, or a church to pastor. You just don't have time to check your messages. "Hold it together baby, you can do this" is what you tell yourself and it has worked all too well; but now, your inbox is reaching its full capacity. You may have messages from childhood pain that have been left unchecked for all these years. Like this woman, you may also have unread messages from the pain of a messy divorce. Maybe yours is from a hurt suffered in the church or on the job. Though you've managed to numb the pain, the symptoms are still affecting your current marriage and your current work in the church or job performance. These messages can no longer be treated like spam or junk mail. They require a response from you. Your tears have been building like a tidal surge behind a floodwall. It's time to let them go. *"They that sow in tears shall reap in joy" (Psalms 126:5).* There is a joy that can only be experienced after you have cried. Respond to your pain, allow the levees of your heart to break, that your tears may flow unhindered. Responding will indeed require you to feel pain as you deal with each message, but God is listening. Your cry is His nociceptor transmitting the message that his daughter is in pain and needs Him desperately. "I cried by reason of mine affliction unto the LORD, and he heard me; out of the belly of hell cried I, and thou heardest my voice" (Jonah 2:2). You've ignored the messages that your heart, your soul, and your mind have been sending you far too long. It's time to respond. You've Got Mail.

While you were sleeping

"And the LORD God caused a deep sleep to fall upon Adam, and he slept: and he took one of his ribs, and closed up the flesh instead thereof..." (Genesis 2:21).

Let's go back for a moment to the genesis of creation. Before God creates Eve, He first puts Adam to sleep. Adam then awakens out of his slumber to see God's handiwork in all her beauty and feminine splendor. He can not attach a label to her based on anything she has done, or anything she's been through. Adam can only declare her to be what she has been from the very moment she was created and while he was still asleep. He calls her Woman. There is a definite sense of awe as he acknowledges the grandeur of her design. She is created from Adam's rib, but without his input or opinion. God did not require them. *"For I know the thoughts that I think toward you, saith the LORD, thoughts of peace, and not of evil, to give you an expected end" (Jeremiah 29:11).* God takes you so seriously, that not one event on the road to your destiny has been left to chance. From beginning to end, every detail has been placed on His desk for authorization. From Eden till this very moment God has never required Adam's signature to approve his plans for your life. So, why do you? Perhaps there are Adams in your life who have been sleeping during God's planning sessions and design proposals. It's time they wake up and see the finished product. You are indeed. Woman!

This is not what I bargained for

> *"For of this sort are they which creep into houses, and lead captive silly women laden with sins, led away with divers lusts..." (2 Timothy 3:6).*

In marketing, it is a proven fact that a person will buy based on emotion, but will then justify the purchase logically. When a buyer cannot find the logic in a particular purchase after the emotion has worn off he experiences a strong sense of guilt or regret known as buyer's remorse. Buyer's remorse is easily cured when the item in question is a flat screen TV or a diamond tennis bracelet. You need only take the item back and receive a full refund of the money you've spent. However, when dealing  with matters of the heart, an ounce of prevention is worth a ton of cure. One cannot simply ask for a refund of time spent on those who are not worth the time. Once the heart has been invested, there is often no refund to be given. You may pull out and cut your losses, but you will have indeed suffered those losses. Time, tears, and trust are all easily lost and yet each proves nearly impossible to recoup. Timothy's use of the term silly is not a measurement of actual intellect but a reference to the fact that women are allowing themselves to be led by their emotions into relationships of bondage. To take heed to the voice of one's own fear or loneliness, or lust is always dangerous because these voices cry out much louder than the still soft voice of patience and are always speaking without the benefit of logic. Ask yourself; Are there sound, practical reasons for the each relationship in your life? What logical justification is there for the time and energy you spend on a particular person? Are your combined efforts creating or producing results that are greater than the individuals involved? Keep in mind, there are some relationships that actually defy logic, and are clearly the Lord's doing; and though they are marvelous in our eyes, they are the exceptions and not the rule. For the most part, your decisions will need to be made with a little less emotion and a little more logic. Also, be vigilant; understand that there are men who are master marketers. These are men who know how to find a woman's emotional buttons and press them

---

> Ask yourself; Are there sound, practical reasons for the each relationship in your life? What logical justification is there for the time and energy you spend on a particular person? Are your combined efforts creating or producing results that are greater than the individuals involved?

---

repeatedly with words and deeds that appear to be genuine at the time but lack the prolonged consistency of truth. If you really want to avoid buyer's remorse in your love life, apply logic first. What does his work history say about him, is he a floater who is always finding and losing great jobs? A master marketer knows how to sell himself during an interview, but lacks the character and integrity to deliver on his promises. As a result, a few months into the job the boss realizes he has been hoodwinked. It stands to reason that if a man can give a masterful performance during an interview, he may also be performing during the dating process as well. Also, don't allow the fact that a man is born again to override your sense of logic. Remember that salvation is not enough, so ask questions. How many churches has he attended; why did he leave? A man who drifts from job to job and church to church clearly has an unstable nature that affects every aspect of his life. The Bible teaches that *"A double minded man is unstable in all his ways" (James 1:8)*. Beware these double minded individuals. One does not have to be a sage of wisdom to understand the old saying; "Fool me once, shame on you, fool me twice, shame on me." Perhaps this woman had been fooled five times. You, however, have a chance to learn from her mistakes. You can break the cycle of guilt and shame and change the current direction of your life. You no longer have to live life in buyer's remorse

> One cannot simply ask for a refund of time spent on those who are not worth the time.

because of decisions made during seasons of emotional instability. At this very moment God is offering a full refund of the time, the tears and the trust you've spent on the wrong people for all the wrong reasons. *"And I will restore to you the years that the locust hath eaten, the cankerworm, and the caterpillar, and the palmerworm" (Joel 2: 25).* They that sow in tears shall reap in joy" (Psalms 126:5). You need only bring him your broken heart and your disappointments as proof of purchase and he will gladly buy them back. "…*And I will rid you out of their bondage, and I will redeem you with a stretched out arm" (Exodus 6:6).* Make a decision today to keep your wits about you at all times. Always listen for the quiet voice of patience and follow it. *"But let patience have her perfect work, that ye may be perfect and entire, wanting nothing" (James 1:4).* Hear God, use the good sense of logic he's given you and you will not continue to say of your relationships, "This is not what I bargained for."

Letting go

"They went out from us, but they were not of us; for if they had been of us, they would no doubt have continued with us: but they went out, that they might be made manifest that none of them were of us" (1 John 2:19).

It's a blazing hot Saturday afternoon. I am sitting in my car (which at he time had no air conditioning) waiting impatiently for my daughter. It's amazing to me that at 11 years old it already takes her an eternity to get dressed. Did I mention the car had no AC? Anyway, I am taking her to the local skating rink for the afternoon session. We're late, and I am irritated. I begin to blow the horn repeatedly but to no avail. Suddenly the front door swings open and slams shut. The thud reverberates through our quaint little cul-de-sac, and somehow in the interim she makes it to the car and begins to frantically press the tuner button on the radio. Finally, she finds the station she is looking for. Apparently she has been listening to a song in the house as she announces with a sigh of relief, "Almost missed it." As I pull out of the driveway, she begins to sing along with the artist. Being a writer I always listen to words before making judgment calls on song selections. So, the frustrated dad gives way to the curious writer as the singer repeats this refrain. "In my mind I'll always be his lady…In my mind I'll always be his girl." I think to myself, if this song is in anyway autobiographical on the part of the artist; I applaud her gift for turning melancholy into melody. There is still, however, the undeniable and ugly chain of bondage rattling throughout an otherwise soothing groove. I wish for a moment that I

could reach into the radio, tap her on the shoulder and say snap out of it lady; he's long gone! Clearly, it is time to let go, but she cannot. His heart is with another woman and yet her heart is still with him. What do you do when the one you're holding lets you go? I wondered how this man could have become so vital to this woman's life that even though he has absolutely rejected her, she is unable to move on. You must refuse to allow your heart to become a shrine for the memory of a past relationship. To be trapped in a moment of time that has passed is emotional bondage. In order to change your future

> You must refuse to allow your heart to become a shrine for the memory of a past relationship. To be trapped in a moment of time that has passed is emotional bondage.

you must leave yesterday where it is and position yourself firmly in the right now of life. Stop trying to rationalize his leaving, and don't waste another day looking for the closure you've been denied. You may have to create your own closure by simply accepting that sometimes, without rhyme or reason, people just leave. Warning signs can be missed, or there may be no warning. I feel John's pain in the above verse. The separation seems somewhat unexpected. He does not seem to have a smoking gun or any particular clue as to why they left. It is always the unexpected blow that hurts the most. John does not see it coming, and so he cannot brace himself. Hurt and confused, John however reminds himself that it was not meant to be, or else they would have stayed. He then realizes their leaving him, though painful, was an eye opener. Their sudden departure made it clear that none of them were for him. Strive to know those that labor among you (*1 Thessalonians 5:12*). Understand that some relationships are temporary while others are permanent. Be aware also that even permanent relationships need to be equipped with what builders call expansion joints. Expansion joints give room for a permanent structure to expand and contract without buckling or breaking as seasons change. Amidst all the uncertainties of life there are two things that are certain: seasons change, and people come and go; always have, always will. In 1 Samuel 16:1, God is asking the prophet Samuel how long he plans to mourn over the loss of King Saul. Samuel's time with Saul as king is over. Saul made his choices and now a decision has been made from which there is no turning back. God then tells Samuel to get up and start being a prophet again. If Samuel can not pull himself together, he will not be in the right state of mind to find and anoint the new king. Many times we make the mistake of trying to build permanent structures on temporary foundations. How long will you mourn over friendships that have ended, or lovers that have left? *"And we know that all things work together for good to them that love God, to them who are the called according to his purpose" (Romans 8:28)*. If you can first accept that what God has allowed is for your good, He can begin to anoint new relationships in your life. Review the mistakes that were made in the past and learn not to repeat them. Change what you can and be at peace with what you cannot, and you will be ready for the new season God has prepared for you.

I built my world around _____?

"It is better to trust in the Lord than to put confidence in man" *(Psalm 118:8).*

I thought it appropriate to leave a blank space in order to challenge you to be both honest and specific with yourself and your Creator.

Who is the well in your life that you have become so dependant upon? What empty waterpot do you carry? Not only did this woman have a what, she—like so many other women — had her share of who as well. With women, the wells are often men. Women are trained for relationships from an early age; usually from the time a girl gets her first Barbie and Ken dolls and begins to play house. Fathers encourage their sons to sow their wild oats, and be in no hurry to settle down;

||||||||||||||||||||||||||||||||||||||||||||||||

There is a difference between needing to be loved and needing to be validated.

||||||||||||||||||||||||||||||||||||||||||||||||

while daughters, on the other hand, are reprimanded for anything less than chastity and monogamy.

Just look in your church, where women outnumber men three to one. Whether God or man, women love to love and be loved. There is, however, a difference between needing to be loved and needing to be validated.

Could it be that the empty waterpots in this woman's life keep her running from one relationship to the next, never learning to be self sufficient? Is it so difficult then to understand that a woman who is emotionally thirsty for love and affection will at times find her self attracted not to the man himself, but to his attraction for her. Her waterpot is empty…therefore she builds her world around the well of his affection. She loves that he loves her. She is thirsty for the "I love you" she draws from him. Having no esteem of her own, she is hydrated by the compliments that flow from his mouth. The single mother raising children finds that her waterpots of authority and finances are empty so she finds a well and builds her world around him. She tells her children to call her well uncle which she prays will slowly evolve into daddy. Her children don't respect him, they only fear him. He doesn't love her or them and deep down she knows it, but her waterpot is empty. She needs this well. This man's heavy hand and steady paycheck are an oasis in the desert of her existence. That is, until it runs dry. Then she must find another or die of her thirst. Understand that the filling of a waterpot is a temporary fix for an ongoing issue. You will always need money; you will always need self-esteem, love and respect. Jesus said that whoever drinks from a man-made well would thirst again. You can fill your waterpot to the rim with whatever it is you're thirsty for, but as long as the source is from without and not from within, there will always be an empty waterpot. Understand that for every brief filling, there is an emptiness that follows. Jesus gives the only real solution to the emptiness. He offers himself as a fountain of living water that would spring up into everlasting life. This fountain was the fulfillment of both her wishes! Now she would never thirst again neither come here to draw! "*He that believeth on me, as the scripture hath said, out of his belly shall flow rivers of living water*" (John 7:38). Having Jesus as a fountain on the inside of you changes your outlook on life. It will give you the confidence to be selective in who you draw from and what you draw from them. In Genesis 14:23, the King of Sodom wanted to be a source for Abraham, offering him the spoils of war. But Abraham said that he would not take so much as a thread so that no man could say he made him rich. Who has been getting the credit for your bills being paid? Who is responsible for the smile on your face or the

> You can fill your waterpot to the rim with whatever it is you're thirsty for, but as long as the source is from without and not from with in, there will always be an empty waterpot.

money in your purse? Whose name is your car in? God wants you to be able to say that no man has made you rich, no man has validated you! No career, no clique, or organization should define 100% of who you are. Where is the mystery in that? Every woman should have a little mystery to her persona. When your source becomes internal your critics will have to wonder why you smile when you should be crying. It is not God's will that you continue to outsource your joy, your peace, or your self esteem. *"I will lift up mine eyes unto the hills, from whence cometh my help" (Psalm 121:1).* If your world has fallen apart because you built it around a well that has run dry, I dare not lie to you. Starting over won't be easy and there is no magic wand to make it all better. It will take prayer, determination, and hard work. For a time you may even feel as though you are dying of thirst in a desert place that was once your life. Weakness, fatigue, and loss of appetite are all symptoms of dehydration; but take heart—this too will pass. Jesus is water in dry places. You will not die but live and declare the works of the Lord! *"Blessed are they which do hunger and thirst after righteousness: for they shall be filled" (Matthew 5:6).* Start looking upward, then inward, and I know will you find the strength to rebuild.

Dropping Your Waterpots

"The woman then left her waterpot, and went her way into the city…" (John 4:28a).

This is to me one of the most beautiful passages ever written because it speaks to the total life transformation that God intends for us. Jesus could have waited for this woman anywhere but he chose to meet her at the place where she is most vulnerable. Standing at the well she is not able to hide her waterpot or the fact that it is empty. "Thou knowest my down sitting and mine uprising, thou understands my thought afar off " (Psalms 139:2). He sees her toting her waterpot from a distance. He watches as she walks with it carefully balanced on her head so that her body supports the weight. Not understanding there is freedom in Christ and that we are not meant to carry burdens, we sometimes search instead for an easier way to carry our issues. The woman with control issues may be overcompensating for the lack of control in some area of her life. A woman who fears rejection will often rudely reject even the most genuine and sincere approach by a man. She may feel she needs to reject him first thinking that given the opportunity, he will do the same. Just as he saw her from a distance, Jesus sees you struggling to balance your issues as you walk. You should be dead by now or in an asylum but you're not. You're a survivor and I applaud you. Everyday you carry issues on your head that would destroy a weaker woman and the average man. While it is commendable that you have learned to survive and function with your waterpots, your movement has been severely restricted. The emptiness you carry has forced you to live your life always mindful of your proximity to your well. *"Casting all your care upon him; for he careth for you" (1 Peter 5:7)*. It's time you learn to live without your waterpot, and away from your well. Be aware, however, that total deliverance does not come without some discomfort or struggle, learning to live without wells and waterpots could mean that you will have to take a second job or go back to school; but God will give you the strength to make it if you trust him. Your children may kick and scream when you announce to them that there's a new sheriff in town and her name is Momma, but the Bible says they will rise up and call you blessed. You will have to learn to love who you are on the inside as well as the outward. If what you see in the mirror does not please you, take the steps to change what you can and accept what you cannot. For years now you've been in survival mode but you can begin to live today! *"He left Judea, and departed again into Galilee. And he must needs go through Samaria" (John 4 3:4)*. Jesus cleared his schedule, just for an intimate encounter with this woman and he has done the same for you! He is waiting at the well for you. There is emptiness inside of each one of us that only Jesus can fill. Be honest with him just as this woman was and tell him about your struggles. Don't be afraid to show him your waterpot. Tell him how heavy it is for you. Let him know how far you've walked and how long you've carried it. He is waiting. *"Come unto me, all ye that labor and are heavy laden, and I will give you rest" (Matthew 11:28)*. *"Casting all your care upon him; for he careth for you" (1 Peter 5:7)*. Tell Jesus how tired you are of the state you're in. You must be thirsty after such a long walk. His word promises that everyone who thirsts after righteousness will be filled. Ask him to give you this fountain of living water that you would never thirst, neither come to here to draw! Finally, Woman believe me; the time is coming and now is: drop your waterpot and go your way!

About the Author

Michael Mines is an anointed preacher, singer, actor, and writer. He has been married to Latricia Mines for 19 years and has been blessed with two children—TyRee, 22, and LyRic, 18. Michael answered the call to ministry in 1999 and is currently a member of True Victory Ministries led by Chief Apostle Sharon and Apostle Aundré Spencer.

Acknowledgements

There are so many people I need to thank and not enough pages; therefore, if you don't see your name in print, know that it is printed on the pages of my heart and my gratitude toward you is without measure.

First and foremost, I must give all glory and honor to Jesus Christ through whom all things are possible. Who would have thought that a liar and a con-man would ever be chosen to carry the truth of God's Word and share these revelations with others. I dare not take any credit, only the mistakes are mine.

My wife and children have been so patient throughout this project, permitting me to lock myself away in my office for hours at a time, day after day. LaTricia, LyRic, TyRee; thanks for sharing me with ministry; I love you all so much! Thanks Pastor Charlotte Stolkes for always being there for me in moments of weakness. Thank you Pastor Jeff Martin for giving me a second chance. I have been blessed to have six true apostles who all being very different have each poured into me out of their unique anointings. Apostle Ruby Turner, you watered that which was planted and God gets the increase. Apostle Barbara Stewart, you ignored my critics and believed in me. Apostle Harriett Askew, you were the first to sow prophetically and financially into this book. Thank you for teaching me to pursue God, to lay on the alter and cry out to him. Apostle Andy Williams, you are a constant source of encouragement and a role model. Apostles Sharon and Aundré Spencer, (where do I start?) you have shown the Mines family so much love. You have given us a place to call home, but more than anything you have called me to a level of accountability that I have never experienced before. You have spoken as true prophets into my life and each word has come to pass. In your humility, you will never blow your own horn, so I will blow it for you everywhere I go. I will tell everyone that there are two true prophets in the city of Hampton, VA. I will say that signs and wonders follow them, and I will proclaim that they are mighty in the spirit, strong in the gift, and humble at heart. There would be no book without the Herculean efforts of Nyla Batts. Nyla literally took *Dropping Your Waterpots* from manuscript to finished product. Then the book died, no one would touch it, and I gave up on it. It sat for five years collecting dust until my sister Ta-ki Morant read the original manuscript, and called me crying in the middle of the night. We talked about it page by page; how it blessed her. And she bought the first copy. But I was stubborn and unwilling to give up on my defeat, smh, until Kim Robinson and my dear Sister Ruth Roman got wind of it and they refused to let it die. They were unrelenting with me about putting it out. They both advertised it on social media without my consent I might add lol, literally forcing me to action. They pushed, and Prophets Dartameon Leonard and Sherry Calhoun declared the Word of the Lord concerning *Dropping Your Waterpots* and here we are today.

Finally, thank you to all my True Victory Ministries family!

For prayer, engagements, or book orders

Email: eldermiketvm@gmail.com
Phone: 757-344-1959

Made in the USA
Middletown, DE
20 July 2022